How about a little quarrel before bed ?

D1385890

By the same author

My God *(Souvenir Press)*
This Pestered Isle *(Times Newspapers Ltd)*
But it's my turn to leave you . . .
Help! and other ruminations
Calman Revisited
The Big Novel
It's Only You That's Incompatible!

Mel Calman

How about
a little quarrel
before bed?

and other diversions

Methuen

A Methuen Paperback

First published in 1981
by Eyre Methuen Ltd
Reprinted 1981, 1983, 1984
by Methuen London Ltd
11 New Fetter Lane, London EC4P 4EE

Copyright © Mel Calman 1981
Designed by Philip Thompson

ISBN 0 413 48830 6

Printed in Great Britain
by Fletcher & Son Ltd, Norwich

This book is sold subject to the condition that it
shall not, by way of trade or otherwise, be lent,
resold, hired out, or otherwise circulated without
the publisher's prior consent in any form of binding
or cover other than that in which it is published
and without a similar condition including this condition
being imposed upon the subsequent purchaser.

To my daughters,

who have become women too quickly for my comfort . . .

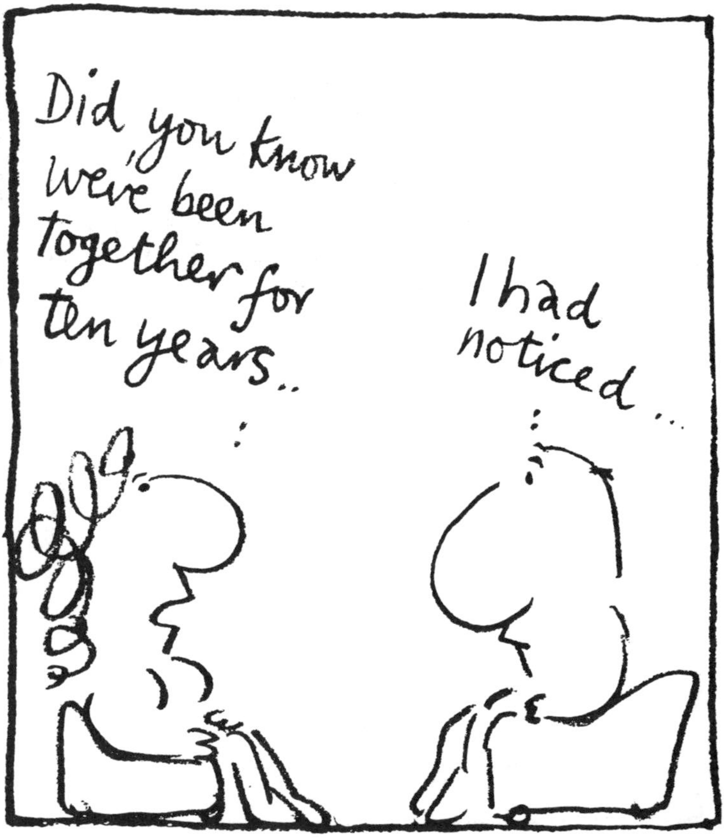
Did you know we've been together for ten years..
I had noticed...

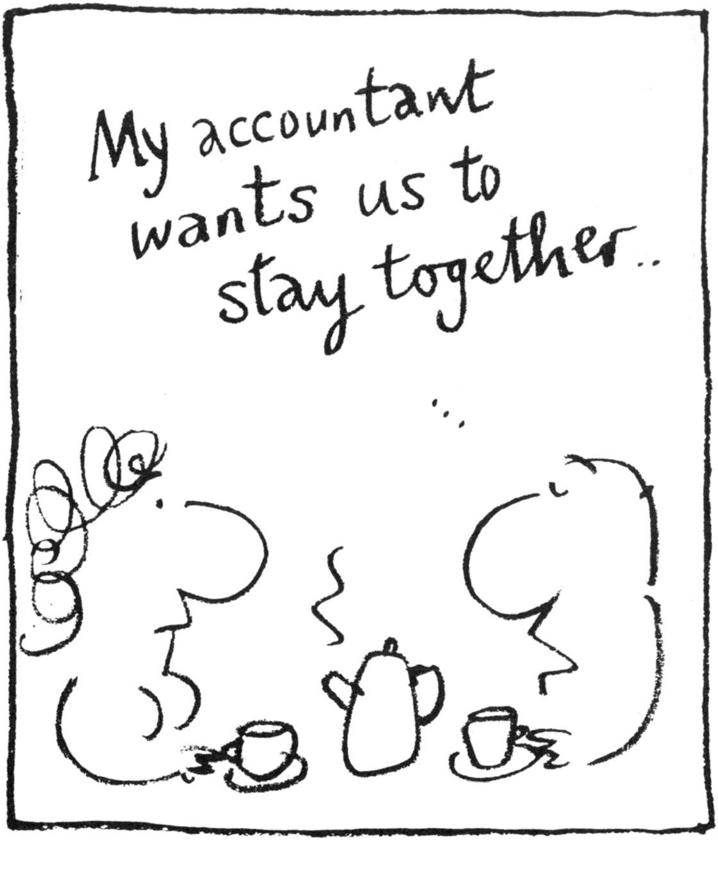
My accountant wants us to stay together..

She gave me
insomnia for my
birthday...

Your boss phoned-
to remind you
that you work
for him..

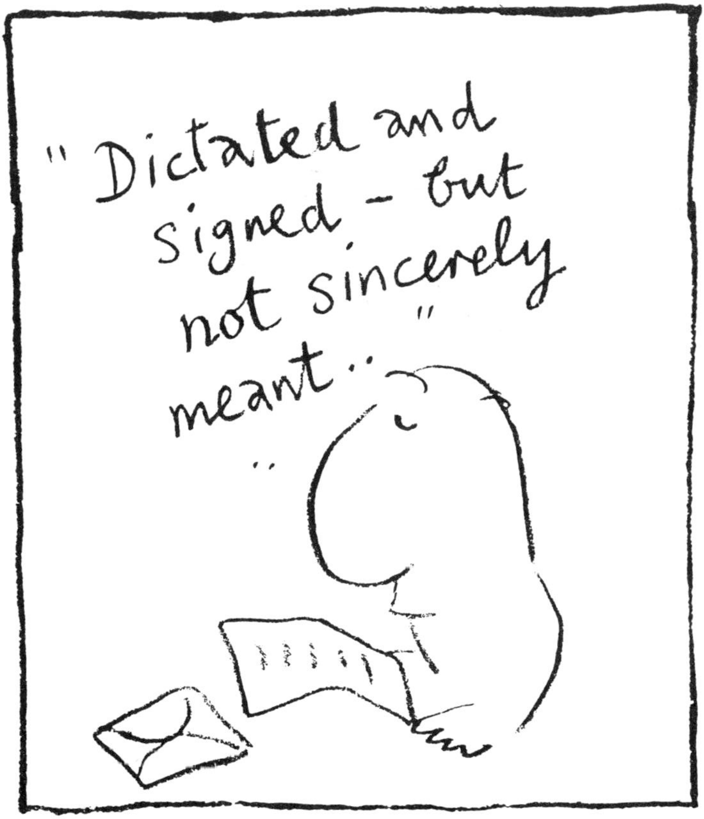
"Dictated and signed - but not sincerely meant.. "

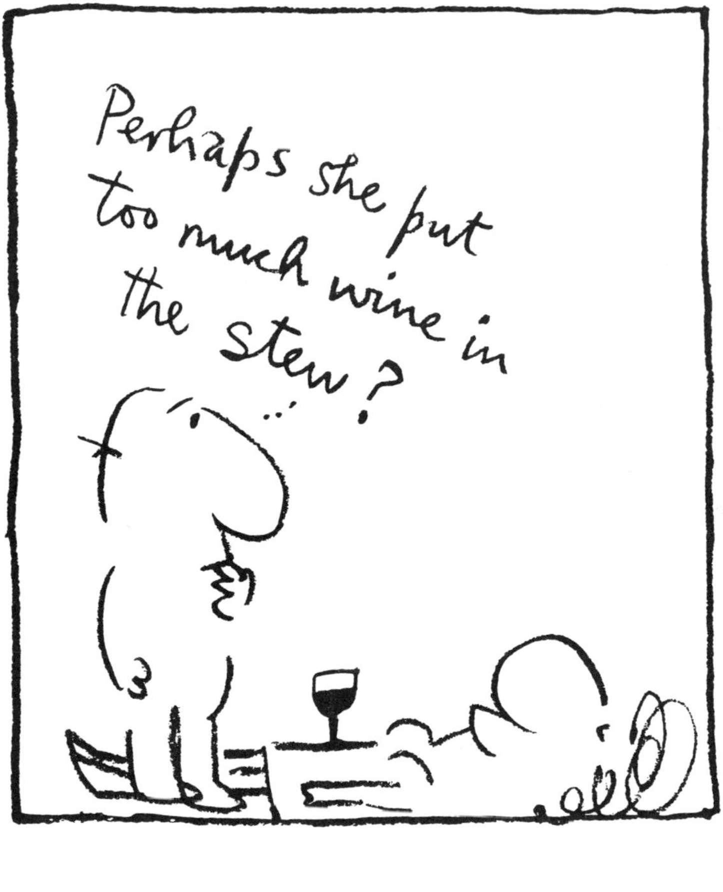
Perhaps she put too much wine in the stew?

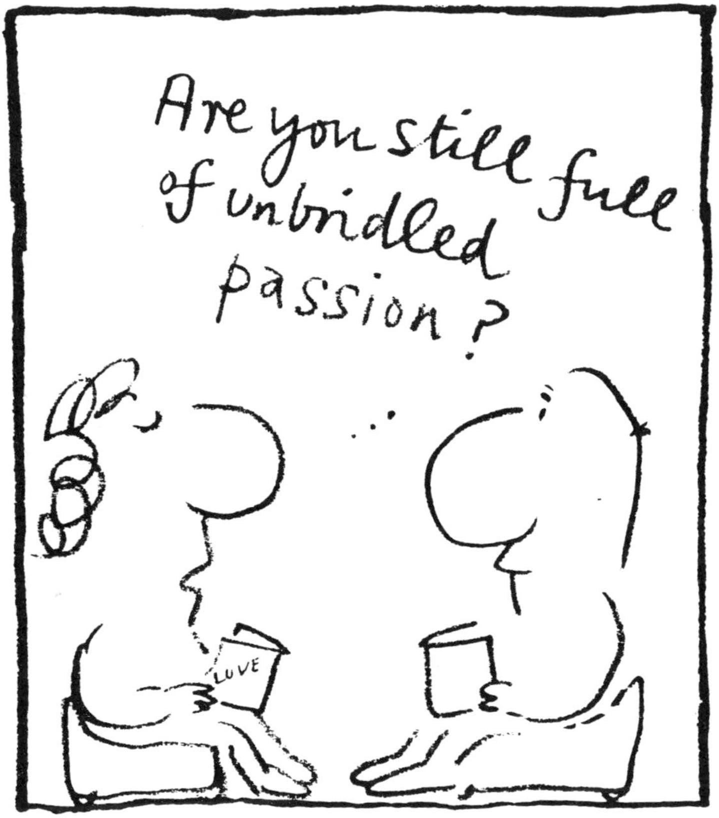
Are you still full of unbridled passion?
LOVE

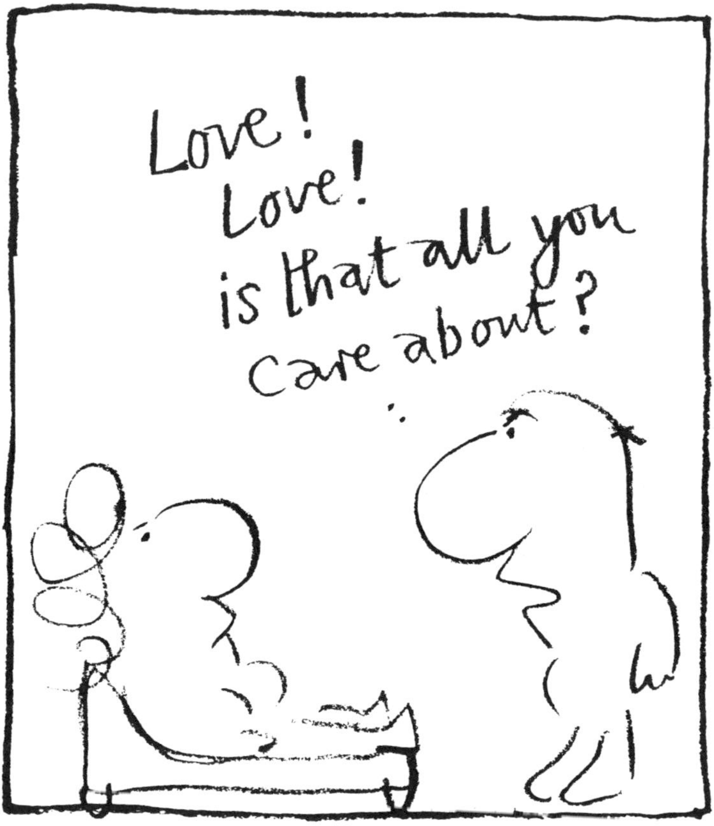
Love!
Love!
is that all you
care about?

You look too pleased with yourself to not be guilty of something ..

Come down -
the ironing
needs you...

With this TOUR you get a free DIVORCE...
TOURS for FUN PEOPLE
HOLS IN THE SUN.

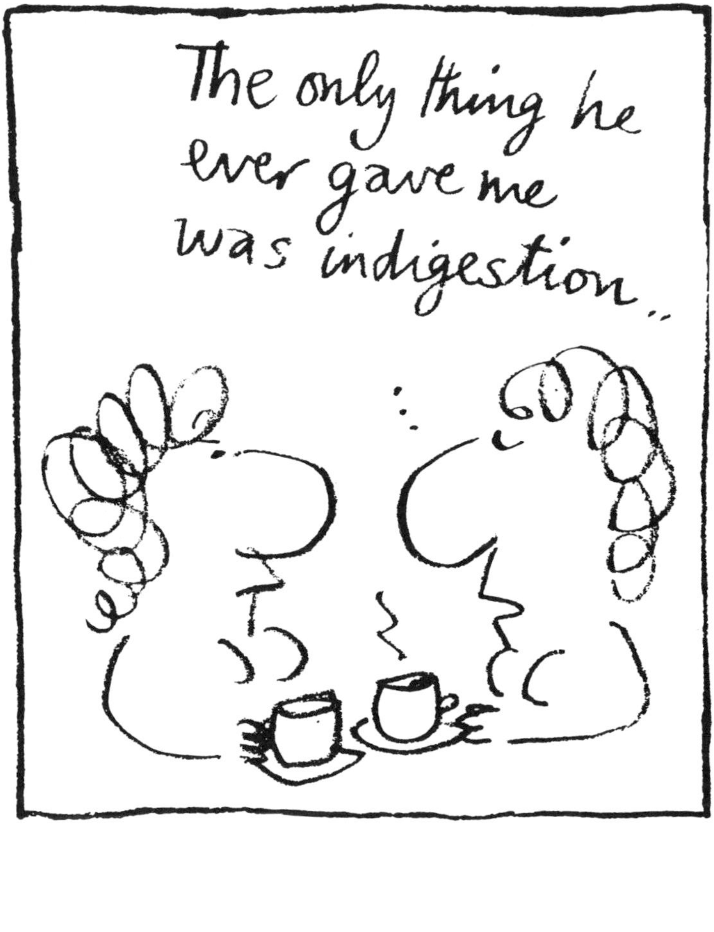
The only thing he ever gave me was indigestion...

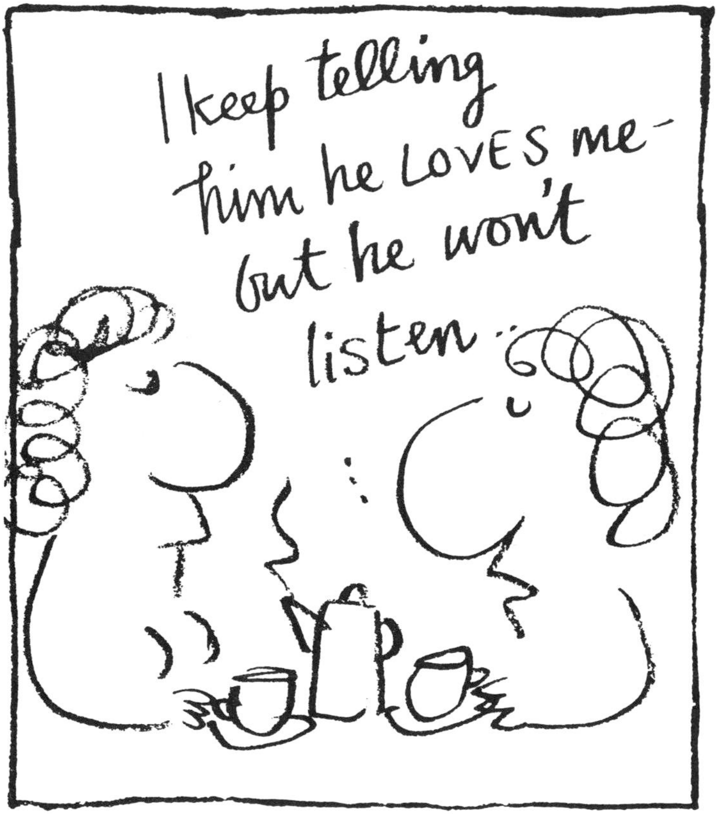
I keep telling him he LOVES me - but he won't listen ...

it's a new diet -
you eat and
I watch ..

WAITER -
bring me a
BANK LOAN ..

Just give me
the bill -
I don't want
to eat

You just asked the waiter for a large bullfighter..
MENU
PHRASE BOOK
PHRASE BOOK

Isn't this romantic?
Except for the prices..

Would you like the bill now or do you want to eat first?
BILL
MENU

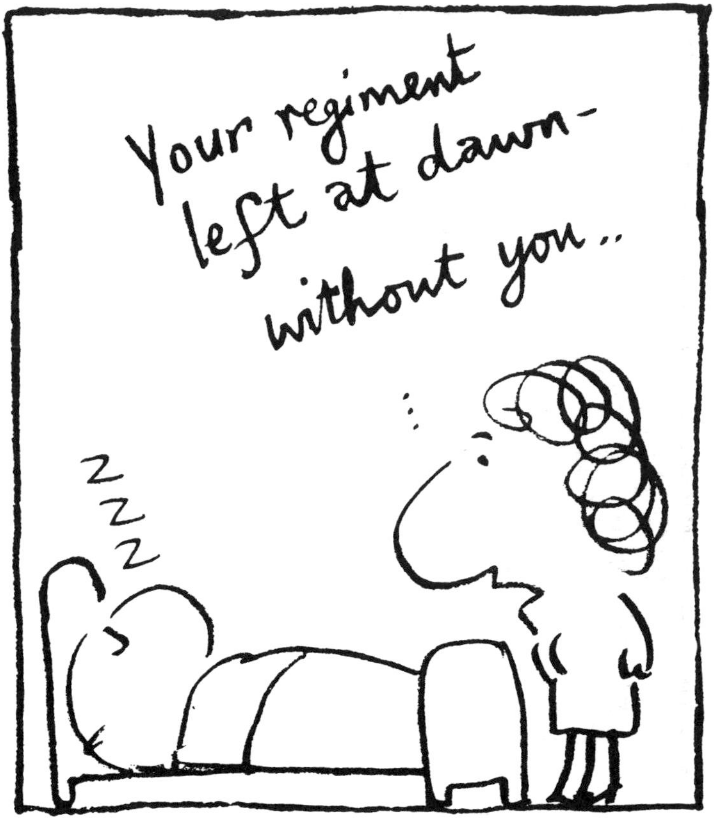
Your regiment
left at dawn-
without you..
ZZZ

I'm tolerant – So long as people don't bug me..

We like
a little walk,
don't we?

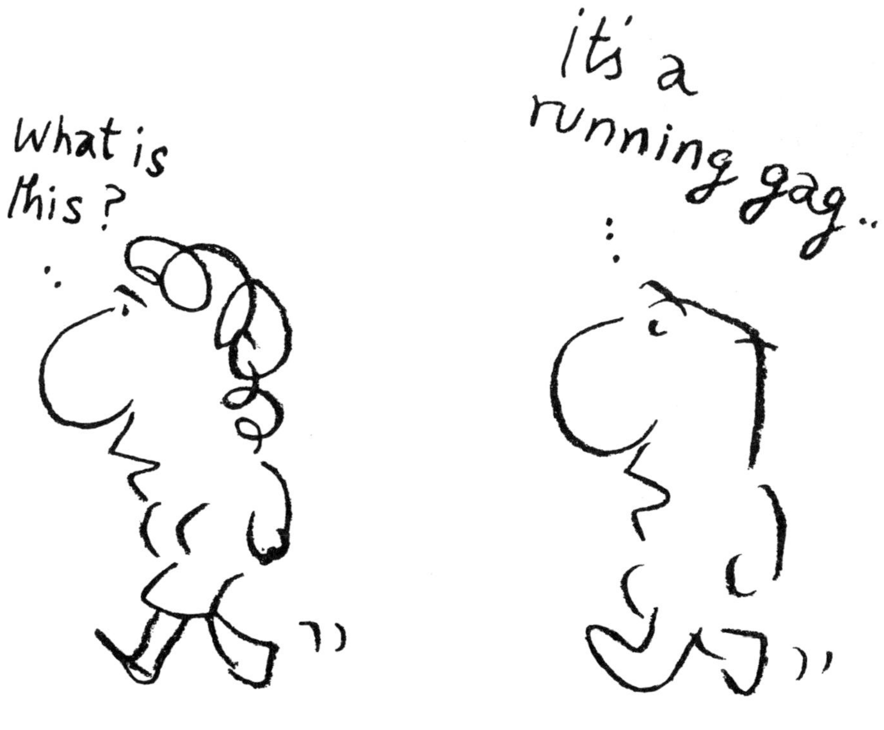
What is this ?
it's a running gag..

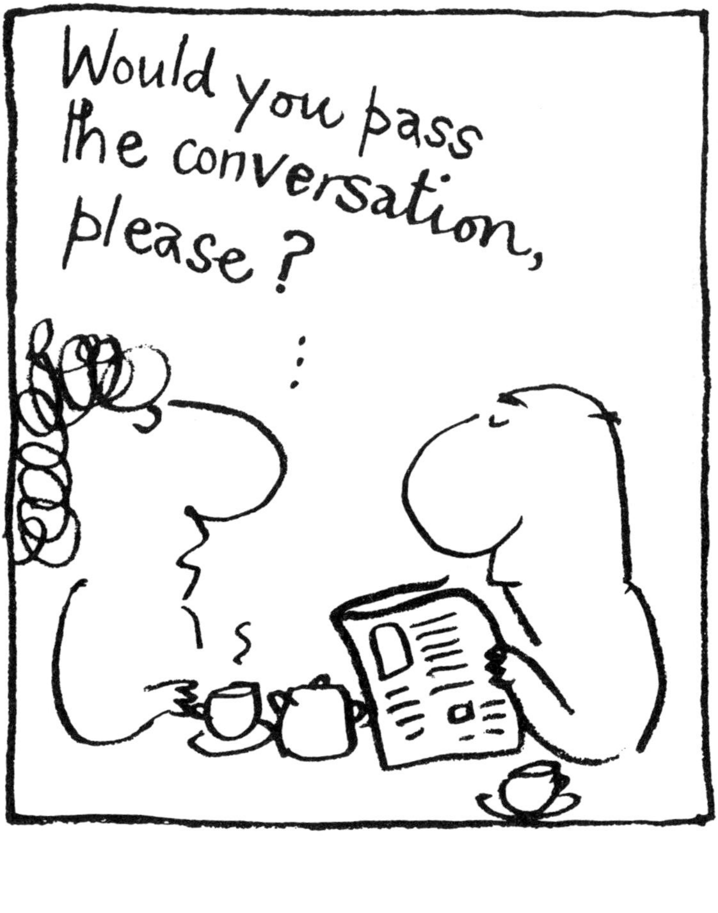
Would you pass the conversation, please?

As I sit here
doing nothing - I am
CHANGING - even if
it doesn't look
like it ...

it's the world that needs the tranquilizers— not me!

Doctor— I'd like a meaningful relationship with money...

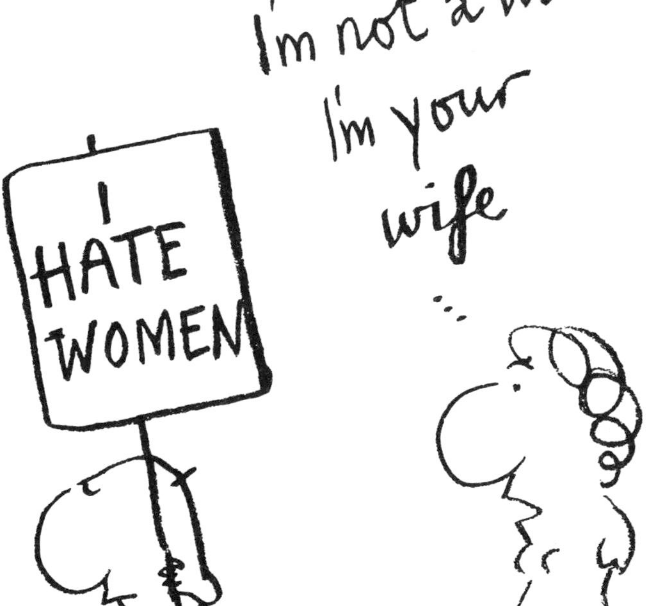
I'm not a woman
I'm your
wife
I
HATE
WOMEN

THANK YOU
for
NOT SNORING.

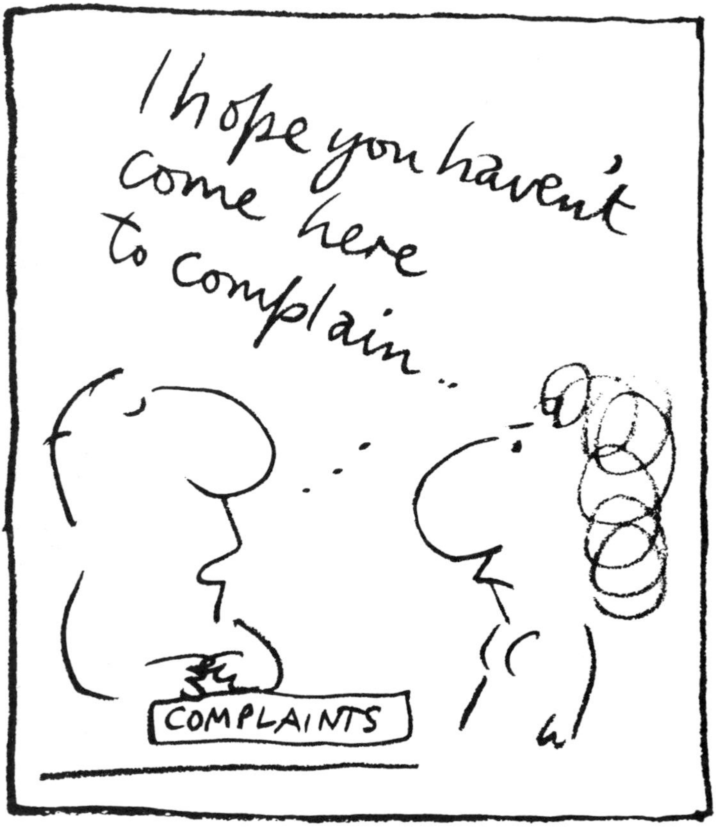
I hope you haven't come here to complain...
COMPLAINTS

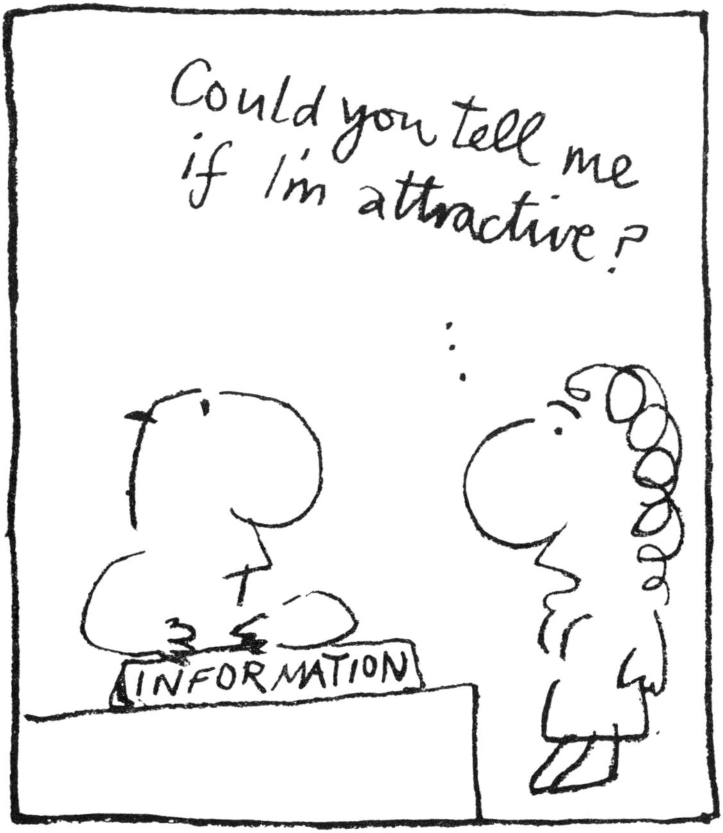
Could you tell me if I'm attractive?
INFORMATION

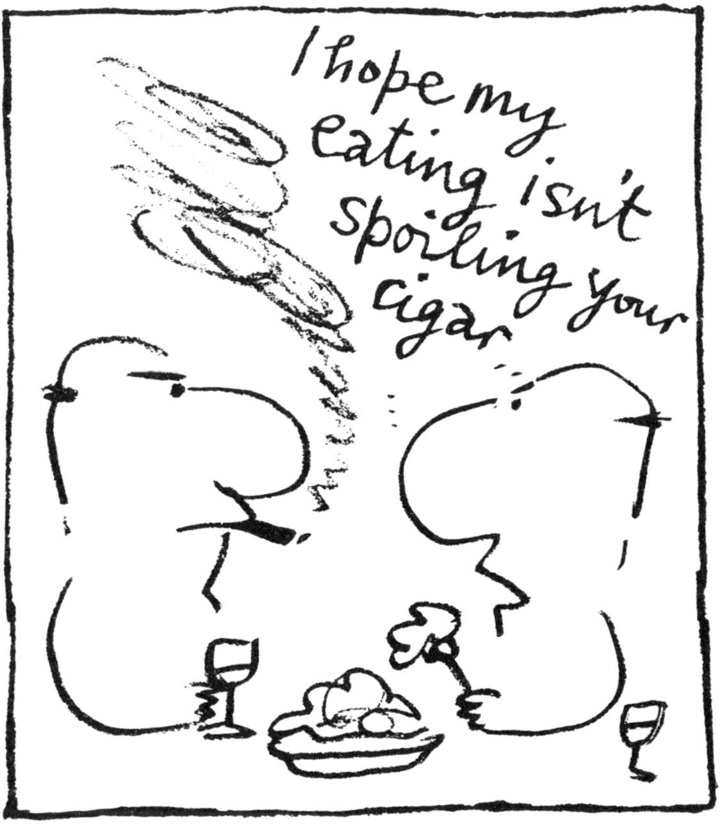
I hope my eating isn't spoiling your cigar

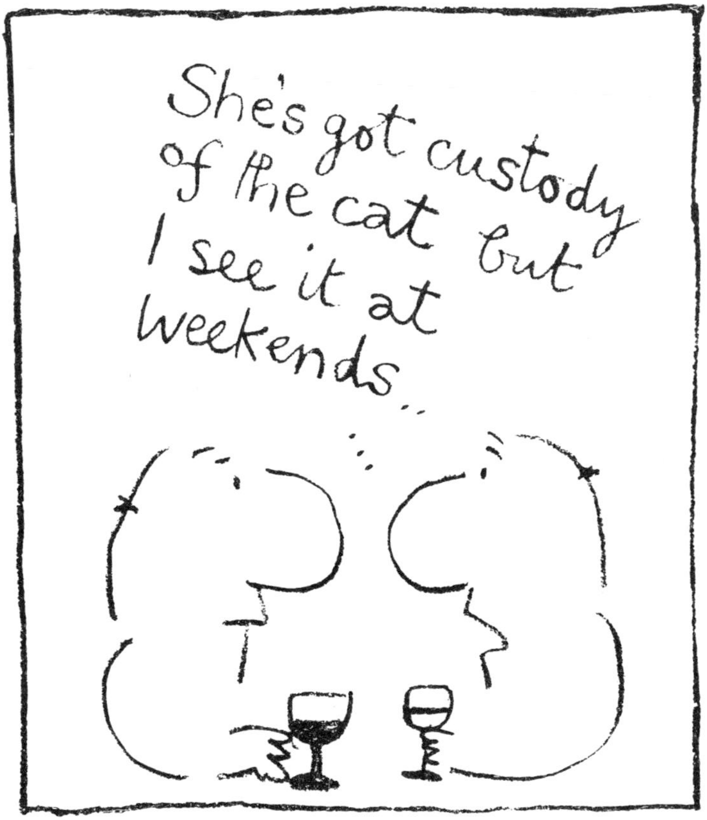
She's got custody of the cat but I see it at weekends...

You're greedy, hostile, depressed, childish, selfish, angry, moody, mean, jealous, difficult and ... IMPOSSIBLE!

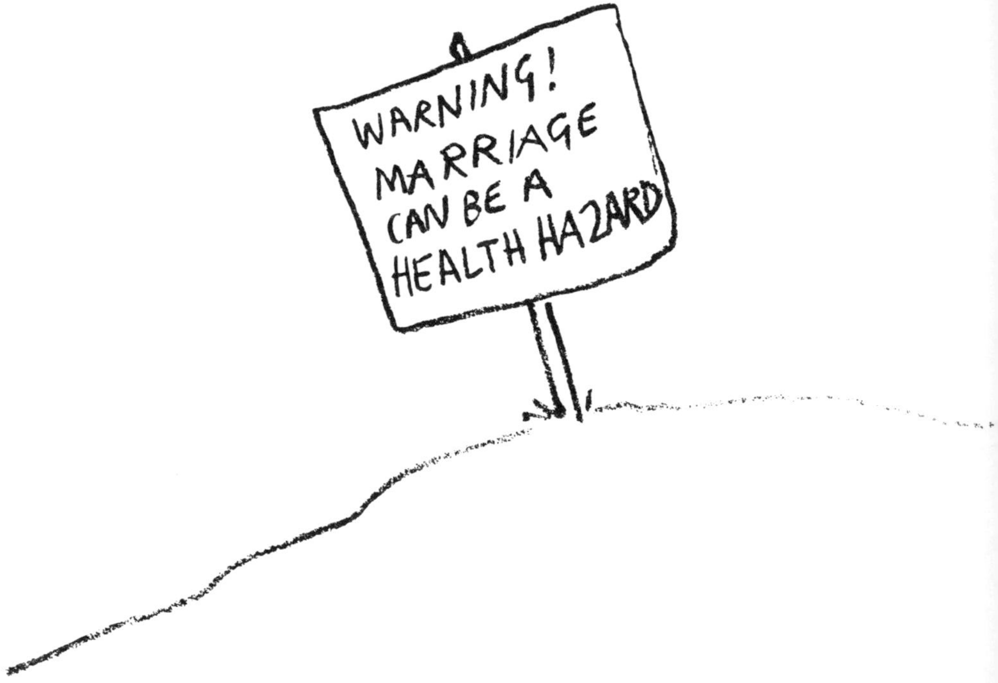
WARNING!
MARRIAGE
CAN BE A
HEALTH HAZARD

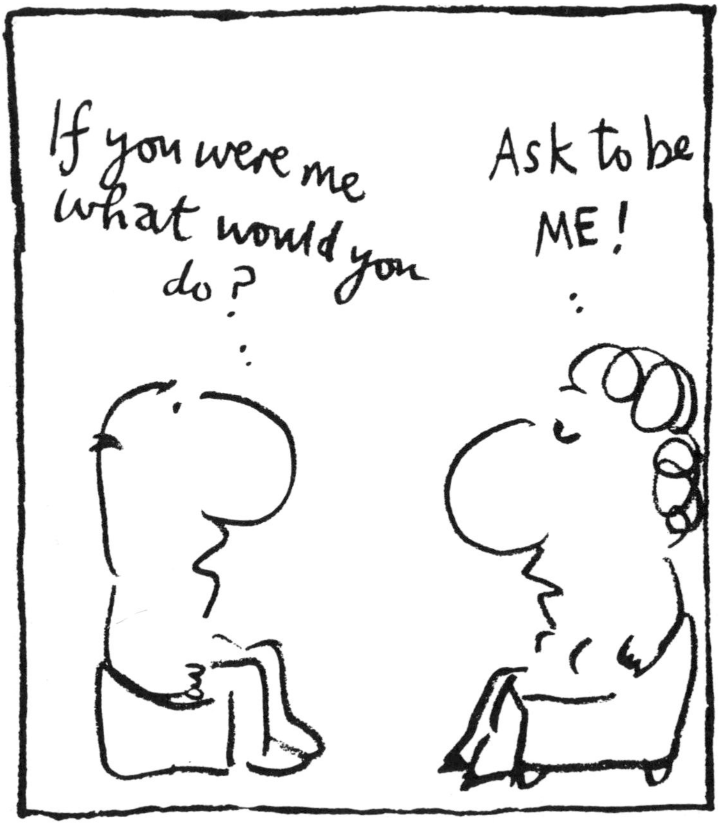
If you were me what would you do?
Ask to be ME!

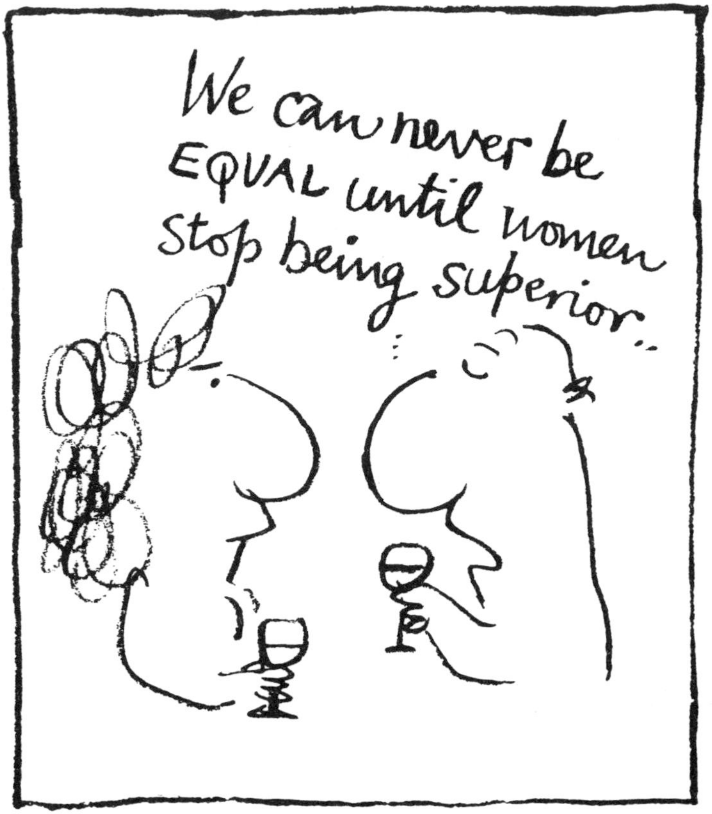
We can never be EQUAL until women stop being superior...

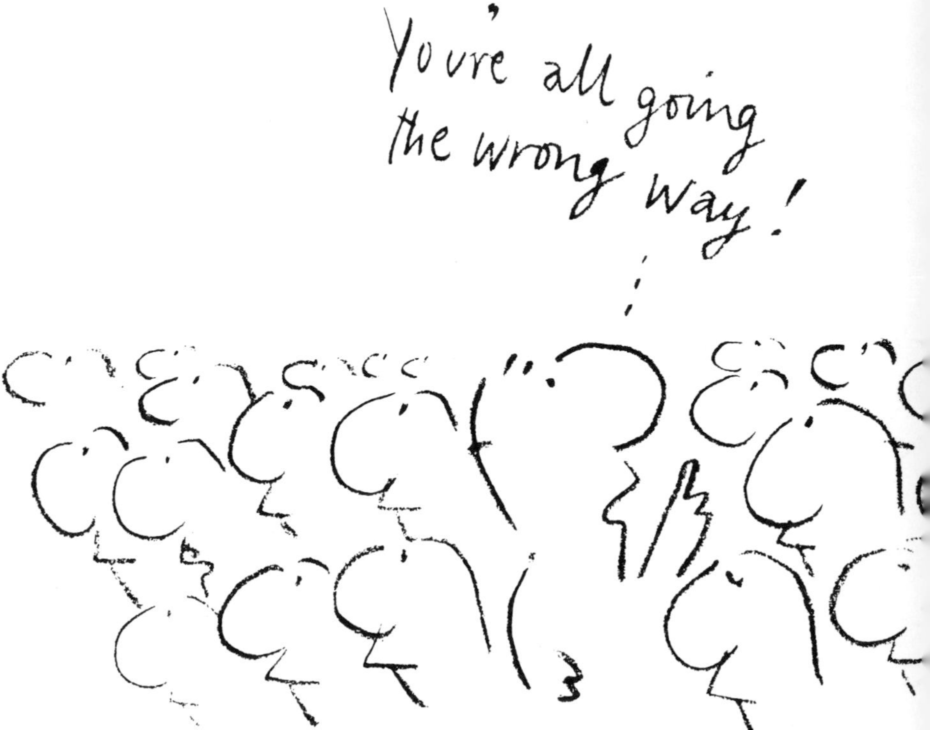
You're all going the wrong way!

Most men are too
selfish to give ME
what I want..

She WANTED honesty.
I GAVE her honesty -
And then she divorced me.

Is this solitude
or loneliness...
:

I'm happy you've got your space – but you're also on the bit of the electric blanket that works

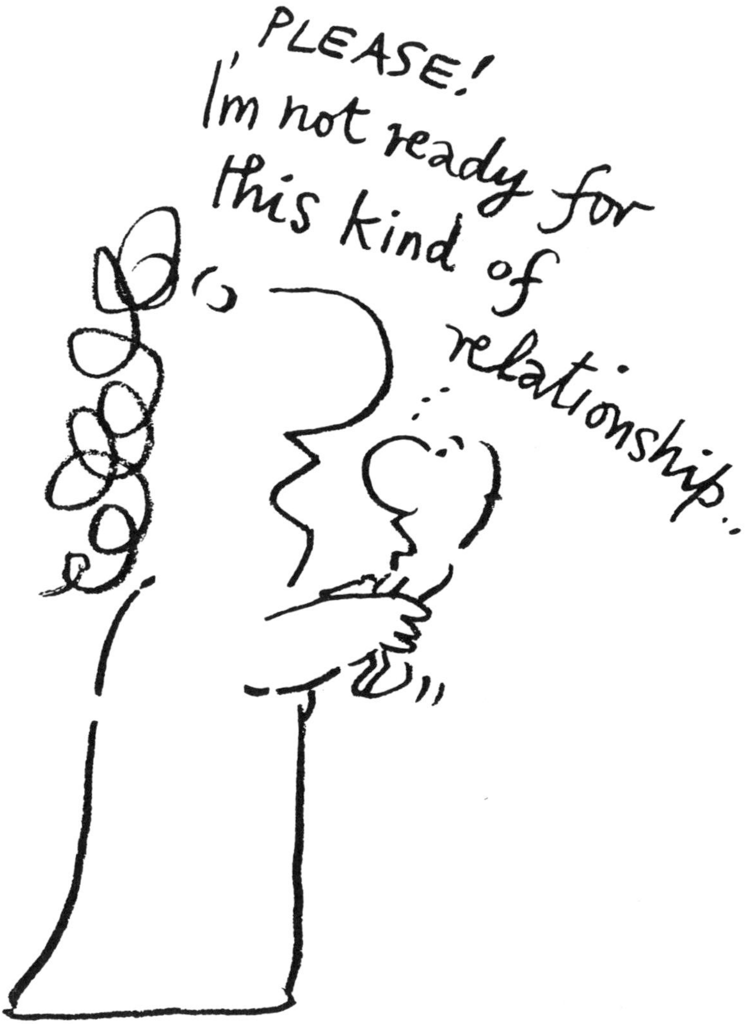
PLEASE!
I'm not ready for
this kind of
relationship..

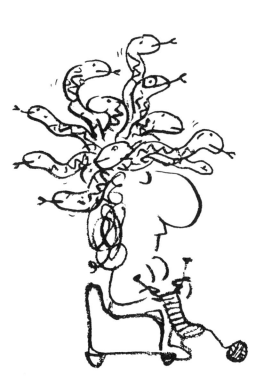

Well?
If I say I liked it- will you promise not to give it to me again?

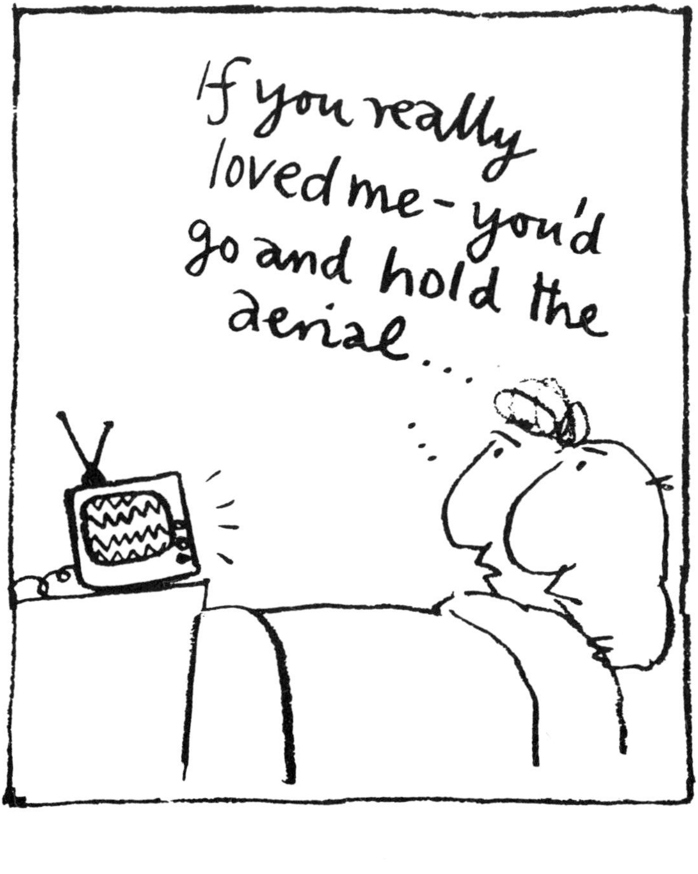
If you really loved me - you'd go and hold the aerial . . . .

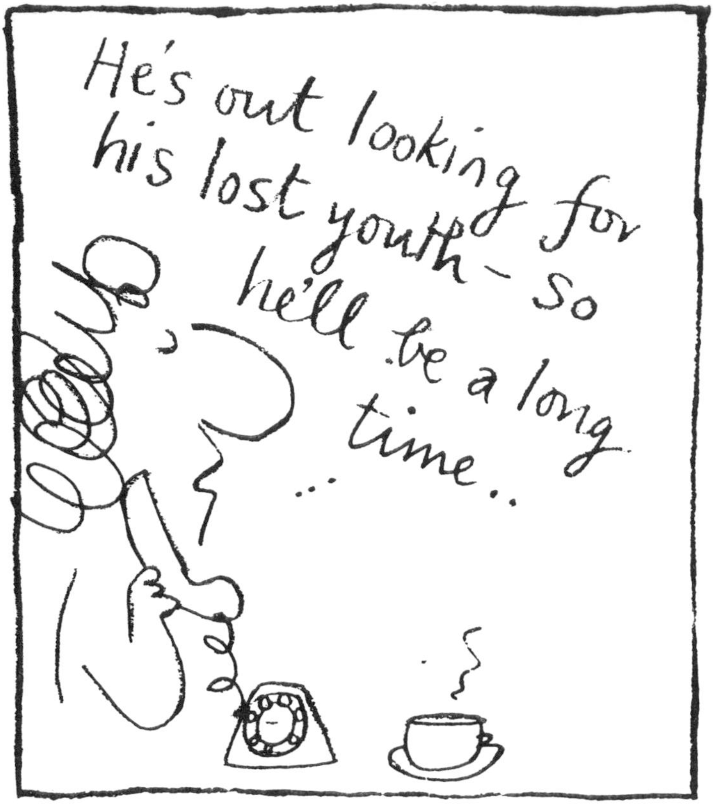
He's out looking for his lost youth - so he'll be a long time...

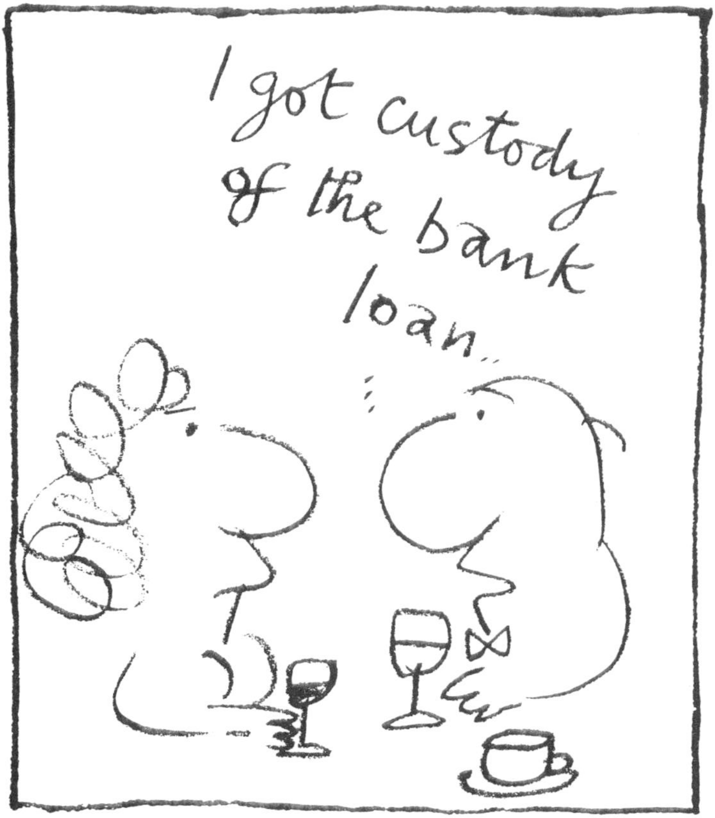
I got custody of the bank loan...

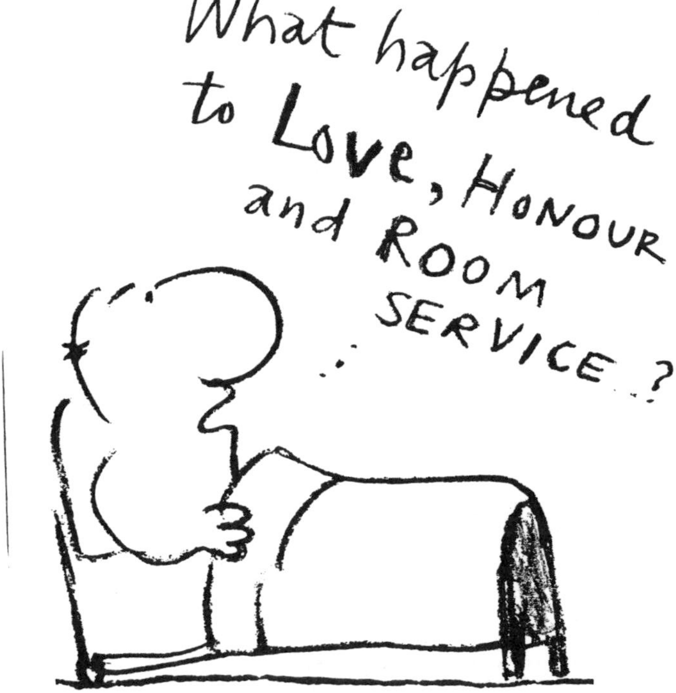
What happened to Love, Honour and Room Service . . ?

I'm taking the
day off from
abstract concepts
today ...

I love people -
within reason,
      of course..

Never try and make a woman
HAPPY – she'll only
resent it..

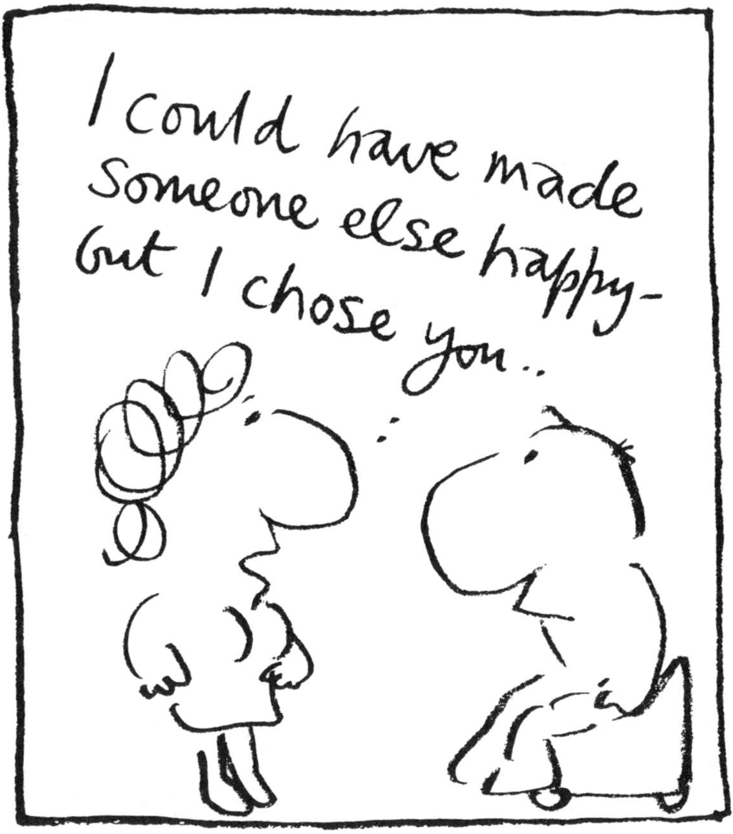
I could have made someone else happy - but I chose you..

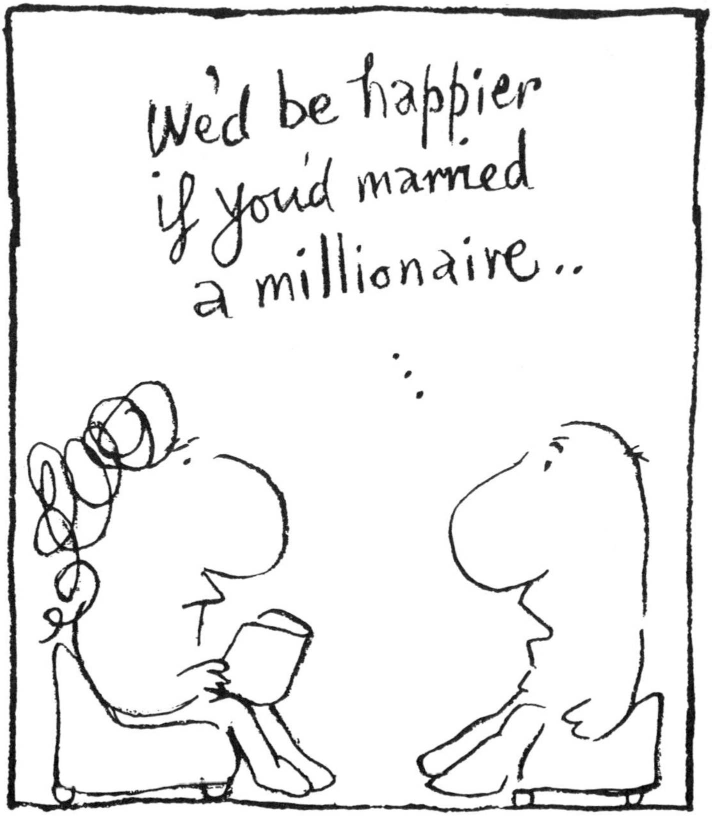
We'd be happier
if you'd married
a millionaire..

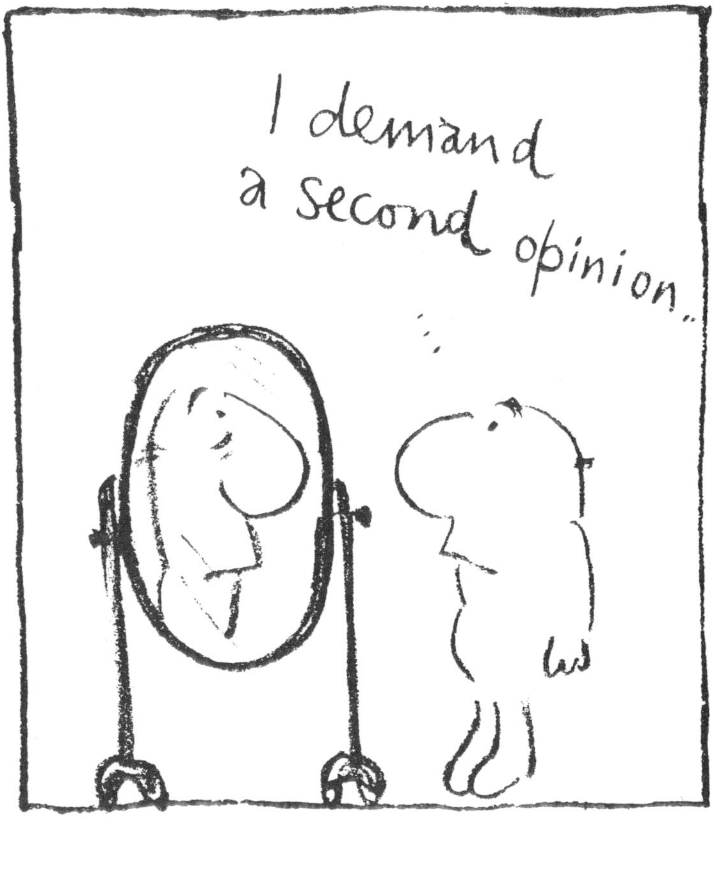
I demand a second opinion..

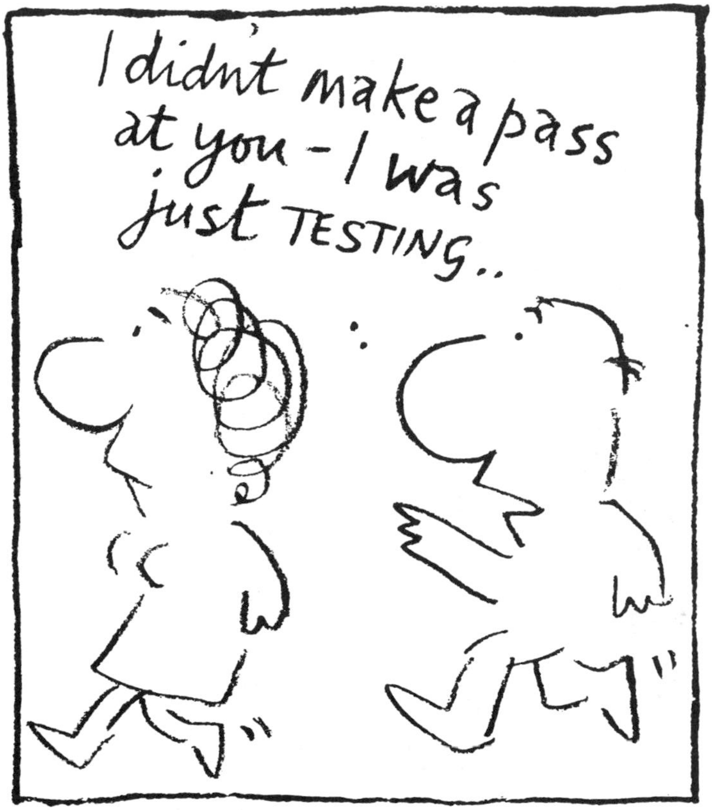
I didn't make a pass at you - I was just TESTING..

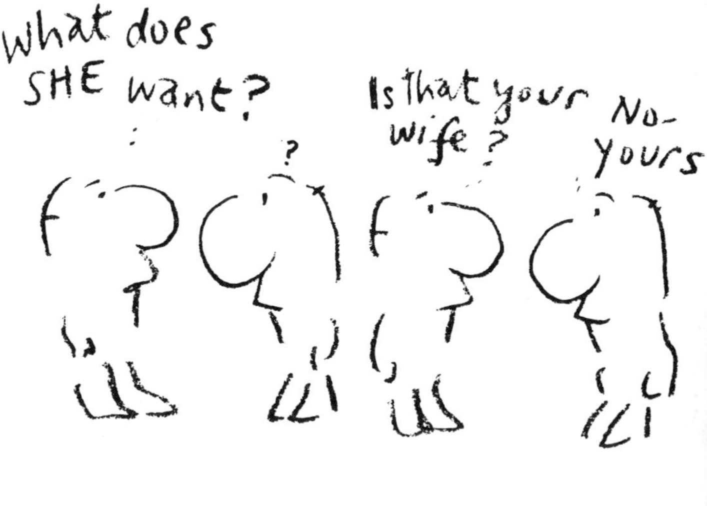
What does SHE want?
Is that your wife?
No- yours

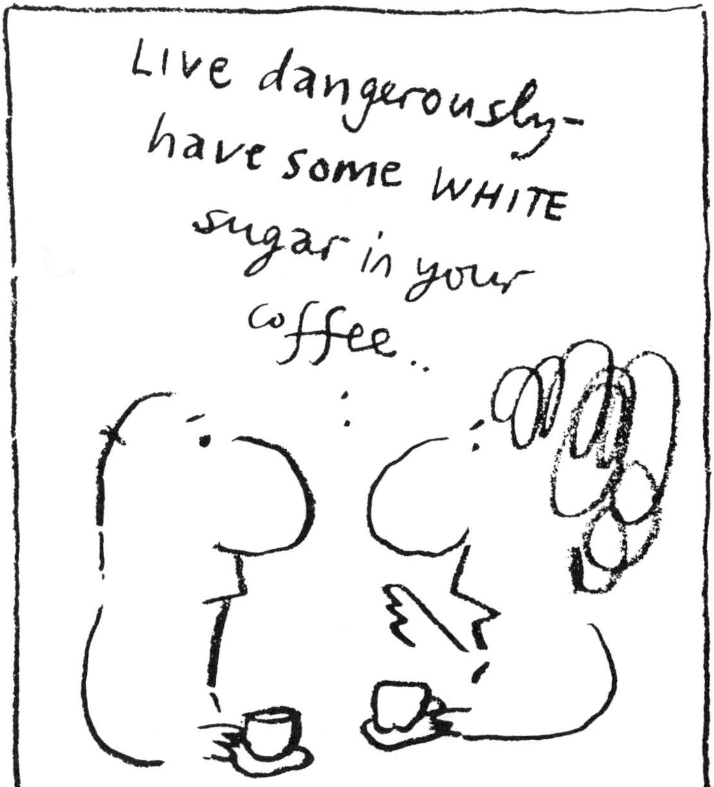
Live dangerously-
have some WHITE
sugar in your
coffee...

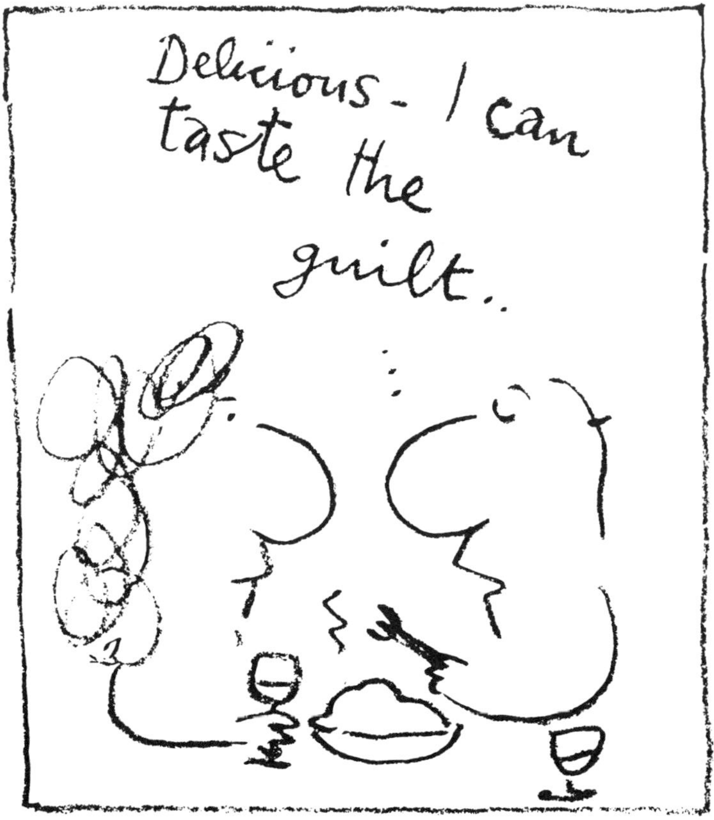
Delicious - I can taste the guilt..